Cover design and digitalization:

Muriel Revisa Designs 2017

ISBN-10: 1542470404

ISBN-13: 978-1542470407

Table of Contents

Foreword

This collection, in its entirety is a declaration of love.

I wrote these poems while tangled in a vortex of feelings, usually beyond the hour of 11pm. This book has been broken down into several categories: love and moments to cherish; grief and sadness; anger, and rebuilding.
Throughout, <u>love is always present.</u>

When I was angry, it was because I had lost you. It was because I didn't want to have lost you. The anger speaks to how deeply I care; had I not cared I would not feel anger. I would not feel anything.
The grief and sadness come from a place of loving you so extremely that it was agony when you were gone.
The love and moments to cherish are what I will carry with me forever. This is what our relationship was and what I will remember forever.
That is our legacy.
When I rebuild, I rebuild a new, stronger person because of your influence and our experience of love.
How lucky I am to have gotten to experience the truest and purest of love. How lucky I am to have had this experience with you. How lucky.

To you, Nikki, in every word, this is a declaration of love. I honour you.

Love

and moments

to cherish

Belonging

You have long dark hair and a long sheer dress and
somewhere along the way
you kissed a girl and felt longing and lightning
twine through your ribs.

You've been called a dyke and you've been called too pretty to be gay;
rejected from each community,
crumpling in on yourself like soft tissue paper torn from a package,
forgotten and
thrown in the corner.

Long hair doesn't protect you from the hate.
Dark and skeletal,
a murder of crows takes the shape of
bigoted men,
they shake their greasy plumage in your face and
you imagine that the slimy feathers left behind are cherry blossoms or soft rainfall,
something less evil than the sheer insolence of it all.

Where do you belong?

Then you met her.

Sunflowers bloom in her eyes on inky dark evenings,
soft flute music slips from her lips, sweet like strawberries,
she takes her love and casts it into every hollow crook of sadness in my being.
Her name is the chime of our gin bottles tapping together
after nights spent laughing in bed.

Our love burns like hot coals, fingers intertwining like vines,

and yet;

She too feels a longing that reaches up from the catacombs of her true self,
a longing stating that she doesn't quite belong.

My baby.

She reaches back towards that yearning, she grasps the hands that were reaching
from beyond prison cells—

She sits in that chair;
the whirr of the hair clippers clacking like spiders legs on a linoleum floor,
she sheds her hair like a snake shedding its skin.

The great hum that had been rattling her rib cage has been released.

She pierces the steel armour of society brandishing a newly shaved head and says

"This is who I am."

The fire of her defiance twists and writhes
through the hatred of the bigots.
It spins and erupts through their verbal poison like bullet spray.

My girlfriend is a beacon.
Her floodlights attract an army of queers from the dense fog of unacceptance.
She makes us feel light,
she is our light,

she is my vivid heart ablaze.

I have found where I belong,
I belong by her side, enduringly.

New Life

I'd been sitting
eyes wide shut
hearing the hammer of the rain
for too long
in that small apartment.

E Boulevard
Granville
Oak
Cambie
Main
Fraser

left turn

41st down to 18th

right turn

through the door

right turn

into your room;

new life.

As simple as hand holding

Each time our hands grazed,
instinct took over
like a sixth sense.
Like clockwork,
it was natural.
Predisposition.
Impulse.
Our hands interlocked;
fingers weaved like baskets,
wine and cheese,
ice cream and the cherry on top,
bowties and jackets,
you and me.

The Emerald City

The first time we went on a vacation,
we were three weeks into dating.
We drove down to Seattle
to see her favourite band;
what better way to connect with someone
than to see their eyes glow
under the neon lights of a dirty bar
front row
listening to the album that defined their 20's?

She spilled her entire coffee on me
not a slight spill where one can look the other way
and maintain the casual conversation;
she quite literally threw the entire thing onto me
and this is when we realized our compatibility:
I cried with laughter ,
she cried with laughter,
as coffee dripped down my leather sleeves.

I begged her to ride the great wheel with me
before I knew of her fear of heights.
She hid squeals of fear as we went around
and around
(I got to hold her hand extra tight).

It was the car ride home
in line at the border
that I crossed borders,
that I told her I loved her
for the first time.

I sent my eternal thanks
to the city that matched my eyes;

I thanked music
and spilled coffee
and being fearless of heights,
for we were about to climb a whole lot higher.

Old Photo

It's an old photo now. It tugs and pulls at the blurred edges of my memory. It almost hurts to look at. The smiles are so genuine; so plentiful and wide. Two women embarking on the journey of discovering each other. Crammed into a fitted bed sheet on the beach at midnight. Blankets stuffed in haphazardly, mostly using each other to (try and) keep warm.

A twin set of black rimmed glasses, and plaid shirts. The same sparkle in both pairs of eyes. She had texted me around 10:30 pm asking if I wanted to go see the northern lights. I was out at a coffee shop studying, heading to bed soon. Suddenly I was seized by an electric energy and my fingers were flying over the keyboard of my phone—yes yes yes I'll come pick you up. Every thought of going to bed was put to sleep.

While we did not get so much as a glimpse of the northern lights (to which she will still protest), I caught sight of the beautiful soul that I was falling in love with. There was still sand in that sheet months later.

Had I known that these same grains of sand were slipping away down an hourglass, counting down to our heartbreak, I still wouldn't have changed a thing.

It is a known fact that a picture captures more than the cumulative affect of pretty words possibly can.

I don't know why I even tried.

Australian

She is as breathtaking as the silver of a paper bark tree
As rough as indigenous land
As intoxicating as the eucalyptus leaves
As enduring as a leatherback's hide
She is as infinite as the tide
As bountiful as the sand
As bright as the southern cross
As tender as a newborn joey

She is as broad as Tibrogargan
As small as her niece
As beautiful as the horizon
As melodic as the waves

She is Australian
The same as I am Canadian;

A mixture of entities
stirring two lives
into one.

Brisbane Pride

I wore a hat that said "QUEER" on the brim, she wore her most reckless smile.

There were hundreds of us gathered in Brisbane, sweltering out in the sun,
melting together.
Pools of glitter gathered at our feet.
There was no music, there was no celebration.

This was activism. This was mutinous.

The systematic trauma of being denied basic humans rights was visible in scars
on arms
on thighs
on shoulders
on wrists
within eyes.

The audacity to be there, the demand to be seen and recognized
was validated in one another through poignant smiles. Was visible
on faces
on t shirts
on banners
on facepaint
within hearts.

Leather dyke lesbians revved up their motorcycles and led the way,
for they started our entire movement, and we followed, as we had through history.

We marched up the street;

it had never felt so important to hold her hand.

I felt tears stab at my eyes as I had never felt so proud to be by her side.
I had never felt so much overwhelming love for our relationship.

We will not wave the white flag of surrender,

as we prefer the rainbow flag of survival.

Letters

For one summer we were apart.
Three time zones,
and the stretch of a country between us.

The evening had a particular moscato shine,
and I made her promise me
"write me a letter every day."

And so, on lonely nights
her handwriting curled around me,
her words held me warm.

Every tear into the paper,
every time I got to break those seals
she was gifting me happiness.

Her syntax
was delightful
Her prose
was sublime

For one summer we were apart
and she
actually
wrote me
a letter every single day.

I still have them all,

the crosses and dots,
the commas and sentiments;
they keep me company
on nights when I can't seem
to read anything else.

Vancouver Changed

Vancouver changed once you were here. There was a subtle shift in the city—
suddenly the most impenetrable rainfalls weren't so bleak as they were spent
laughing, arm in arm on our way out on Halloween. Suddenly every love song on
the radio was about you, the lyrics coiling their way around our hearts like a spring
tightening, ready to erupt like a volcano; the ashes falling around us like light
snowfall. Suddenly places that I had never given a second glance became full of
meaning; red lights became not a bother, but a chance to kiss. Old places of horror
and seclusion were reclaimed. The smell of the bar, the stale beer and quiet
desperation no longer reminded me of my abuser but of us; choking on cider with
open mouthed laughs. Suddenly my apartment became our apartment. Photos of
the best friend who stopped talking to me were replaced with photos of us that
spoke to me. Long nights went from lonely to lovely; busses went from being
miserable to a place where relationships are formed and I love you's are spoken for
the first time. The northern lights became an opportunity to wedge ourselves into a
fitted sheet on Spanish Banks beach and stare at the sky for three hours—seeing
not a colour in the sky while freezing to death yet seeing all the pigment in your
complexion and feeling warmth under my ribcage. Suddenly, Joey's on Burrard
was the most meaningful place in the world. Revolver became the cafe that I now
associate with your mother, where we sat huddled from the racket of the rain and
footfalls outside. Lovers on the street are no longer the source of my sickness, but
your absence is. The mountains were no longer monuments to admire from afar,
but were to be conquered, photos of my legs around your waist to be taken at the
top.
Vancouver is now a place that I want to live, not a place where I beg to die.
Vancouver changed once you were here, and so did I.

Moments

Collectors retain what is most valuable to them,
keep objects that they desire or deem precious.

I've been collecting humble moments with you,
keeping them unscathed and pure in my mind.

Like the way your skin feels when you're just waking up,
soft and warm.
Or the way you smell in that velvety part of your neck.

Like the way you would gently push the warm bath water
over my back and shoulders so I wouldn't be cold,
and the moment you sang to me tangled in bed for the first time.

I hold onto the instant that you put me on your back
to carry me out into the lake,
you dove in while I screamed with the touch of cold water.

You sat with me and my grandmother,
and asked her questions about my heritage over tea.

You kissed me encased in the embrace of
one of the world's largest trees.

I recall the burst in time as your face changed
when you saw your mother who surprised you
from the other side of the world.

The way you would meet me in the park
to lie there and do nothing,

and the first time you managed to stop on skates,

is etched in my thoughts.

I remember how you always packed an extra tea bag for me,
and the way you danced with me on the cruise.

I looked up and saw you at the finish line of my third half marathon,
I looked up and saw you as I graduated university,
I looked up and saw the room strung up with fairy lights and cried.

A moment that will never leave me:
you kissing me
    in public
as I got on the bus after our first date.
It was the first time I knew
that someone was **proud**
to be with me.

The post secret show was a moment of clarity,
bloody and raw, as we delved further into one another.

I remember when we skated on top of a mountain,
and the weight of my body against yours when
we finally sat down after moving into our first
east Vancouver apartment.

I remember
the way you looked at me as I first performed poetry,
something I would not have had the courage to do
if I didn't see you in the (small) crowd.

The perfect goodbye to the city where we fell in love
was to fly over Vancouver in a sea plane.

Each moment I cherish,
like how you would
always kiss me goodnight.

Collectors retain what is most valuable to them,
keep objects that they desire or deem precious.

These moments my dear are my greatest collection,
that I will cherish into eternity.

Toothbrushes

And suddenly there were 2 toothbrushes in the cup on the bathroom counter.
I realized that's when it became home.

Like Wine to Fruit Flies

My two front teeth are crooked. My face attracts pimples like wine to fruit flies. In grade six I wouldn't wear T shirts to school because my arms are too hairy for a girl. I have a mole in the middle of my chest and I've always thought,
I would look good topless, if only.
If only it weren't there.
Small insecurities, lurking in the background, following like a shadow, and I, Peter Pan, wish to avoid it.
Wish I could rupture the raven seams cradling it to me.

A lifetime ago, these snickering little (big) thoughts took up residence in my brain and trashed the place. They run the dwelling in my skull, shitty asshole tenants that I can't kick out.
Seemingly out of nowhere, budding from a right swipe in a phone app, a silver-tongued maiden came along and crammed an eviction notice down their weeping throats.

She gently strokes my mole and muses;
the most lovely pieces of wood earn their true beauty in the knots. The most ornate, the most exquisite masterpieces are carved out from wood bursting with the originality and curves of the knots. This mole is yours.

I thank tinder of the wood and app variety. I can't stop seeing that mole as a knot in the wood of my hard body. Adding to the beauty, the uniqueness.
That woman is a craftsman; and she showed me that the doubts my shadow cast upon me were nothing but a rain shower, tokens of true beauty. Nothing but small whispers on the wind remain of the past. I can barely hear them.

Shadows don't, as it turns out, exist without the sun.

Intertwine

trace you
feel your warmth
chest to chest
your name sounds like
the light buzz
of patio drinks
you feel like Sunday morning
inhale you
exhale me
intertwine

smell the gin
smell your perfume
bass lines ripple
my perception;
you ripple
my brainwaves
your brainwaves
intertwine

volume up,
blankets down
lips touch
one body ends
where the other begins
hot showers
intertwine

you are the
first hour of a road trip
you are
the surprises found in a spring jacket
you are
the moon
i am
the moon
intertwine

you feel like clean bed sheets
rainy hair
swooping stomachs
the peak of the arc
high
to low
go down
intertwine

seize me
clench me
grasp me
pluck me
intertwine

Headlights

I used to pace the dark streets
alone
screaming at my insanity
numb to the danger;
the cold sidewalk
digs into my cheek
and
I barely feel it.
I've been here so many times before:
I am callused.

It was a night like any other:
dejected
on the ground
but this time headlights shone
into my black eyes;

that was you my love.

You took me home.

Nature's Beauty

It was but a fraction of time.

I looked at you, standing there on the deck of the ship;
we climbed the stairs to be lost in the wind,
to be alone together.
You wore a blue top with white flowers on it;
I wore your denim shirt
that you gave me to keep warm.

A mojito was in your hand,
it sparkled in the sun.
I marvelled at the impossibility of such elegance;
we were surrounded by the shimmering ocean,
by the rich warmth of the sun,
by nature's beauty.

And by nature's beauty,
I mean you.

I simply saw you
and I couldn't stop thinking
she's so pretty
she's so pretty
she's so pretty.

With Laughter

We had been dating for one month when her birthday rolled around,
and I rolled ideas through my head:
How big do I go? What is too much or too little?

I decided that you can't go wrong with a nice dinner out,
so I chose her favourite—thai
it was a fusion place
(or so I thought)
but what we were served was not thai.

We were served sludge
covered in mini shrimps that she detested
as well as extravagantly questionable fish
(she also hates seafood).

I thought I could salvage it,
I asked to have a candle put in the dessert
"No."
It became clear why
when they brought out a bowl of liquid,
a syrupy gruel-like disaster;
a candle couldn't have stood in it,
it would have sunk like quicksand,
like my sinking feelings.
I blew it.

I apologized many times.
My intentions were the kindest.

Then we laughed,
and we laughed.

That's when you know
that this is the kind of person
you can spend the rest of your life with:

these small mishaps become the story,
they become hilarious,

they become better than the original plan.

Some people don't have the ability to laugh like this.
What may have turned to be a forgettable night
is now imprinted into our memories

with laughter.

The Forest

I never thought I could do it. This whole moving across the world thing. How could I be so far from my family? What if there's a disaster? What if I get homesick? What if my grandparents fall ill? What force of nature could possibly pull me away?

Turns out, she is a force of nature.

She is a wild thing. She is a forest that has grown dense around my heart, protecting it. Nurturing it. Her roots wrap tightly around me, bury themselves down into the marrow of my bones. Her branches cradle me. Strong boughs; smooth. I do not fear they will break. She lifts me so high that I can see the whole world from up here. That babbling creek running by? That's her voice, singsong and lilting, whispering words of eager fondness. The bark, rough yet gentle, cases me in; holds me with a passionate fascination. Winds gently roil, hands turn to soil.

I have always felt most at home in the forest.

Water

When
the world
decided to burn
me at the stake,

she showed up
with buckets
of water.

Things I thought I knew

I thought I knew everything about her. We had been together nearly 2 years after all. We had shared secrets so intimately, danced away trepidations and fully accepted each other for who we were. I had heard elaborate stories of the other world she held inside her, and with these images I felt I knew her.

But there is something about taking a 14 hour flight to her homeland; something about riding along the bicycle paths over which she careened as a kid.
Last night I took a bath in the same tub where she took her first soak as a baby. I could almost hear the coo of her mother's tender voice and my loves small gurgles.

I have been sleeping in her childhood room. I am walking through her firecracker memories years later.

We attend family gatherings, we share whispers as an unexpected guest shows up. She hasn't seen her stepsister in years.

I am immersed in this other world that used to simply colour my mind in beautiful still frame pictures.
I am discovering a love deeper than the ocean and more bountiful than life.

And to think; I thought I knew everything about her.

Darkling

Part of my spirit harbours a
darkling.
Some nights she could tame it,
other nights she couldn't.

Don't go to sleep my dear,
for we don't know when
the incubus

is coming.

Unleash the
fireball that you are
and conquer my dark side.

Thank you.

You didn't stop loving me.

Thank you.

This Woman and I

Have stood atop the Sydney Harbour bridge,
    sailed the inside passage of Alaska,
    traversed sand dunes in Death Valley,
    stumbled through bitter cold winters,
    lay on beaches vast,
    been atop the Rocky Mountains,
    gone from the coast of Canada to the coast of Australia,
    run through fields of tulips,
    bathed in hot springs, in frigid lakes,
    touched the biggest trees in North America,
    supported each other through university,
    laid in luxury, and slept on the ground,
    drove up the sunshine coast,
    been to weddings and vineyards,
    celebrated the strip of vegas,
    carved pumpkins and turkeys,
    sat under Christmas trees hand in hand,
    drove from Sydney to Brisbane,

but by far the most exotic place,

the most intoxicating place we have visited,

is each other.

Three and a half months

My family vacation to Portland will forever be
carved into the tunnels of my memory.
It was the time of caterpillars to butterflies,
as we began to grow into us.

I sat in a cabin in the woods,
surrounded by family laughter,
as I typed, day by day,
recounting my adventures to you.

You would always reply, and I started to
be able to catch a glimpse of
this rare painting that was your life.

Paragraphs stacked on paragraphs,
understanding and connection,
you were pitched at me
full speed
knuckleball.

We spoke for three and a half months
without meeting once,
but
let me tell you,
I felt you well before I ever met you.

You had already weaved your way into my heart
with your words.

Those three and a half months
changed everything.

Her

       She takes my thoughts on journeys through time and lies them to rest in truly enchanting places.
She makes the harsh concrete outside feel like a luscious bed of moss under my feet,
the sound of cars a beautiful waterfall, softly caressing my fingers.

       She has an ability to make the world disappear, and suddenly we are lying down gazing at the hazy sun in our secret mountain oasis.
She lets me grow, like a bright green vine climbing up the mountainside,
interlacing around the stones like our fingers intertwining among each other.

       She makes the apartment turn into a field of blossoming flowers, all of which smell like her;
the pinks and yellows and purples of petals all mingling to create a plush carpet of bliss.
She speaks and it's a soft wind, gently cooling me and lovingly tucking my hair behind my ear.

       She makes the roughness of other people dissolve like particles of sand under my toes,
the sadness swept away in the swirling sapphire rivers of her love.

       She has eyes that light up like a full moon at the turn of the month, her sunflower gaze pulling me into its infinity.
       She had me loving her long before it was okay to say so, as her hands smooth over me like the soft waves of the tide.

       She frees my mind from the harshness of the world,

and suddenly the ordinary is

       anything but.

She

She's the nicest thing I've seen.
She is the antagonist to the poison that once lurked within the confines of my skull.
She is the anti-venom when the world bites me. She makes me laugh until it is
truly painful and I beg her to stop.
I like it when she doesn't stop.

She is my green tea in the morning (the most important part of my day).
She is the green of my eyes (my favourite colour).
She slashes stereotypes in half and fights back against the ignorant. She is all my
favourite songs on loop.
I like it when she sings to me.

She is the taste of pine in my mouth when she mixes unpolished gin drinks. She is
the vice grip that surrounds my hand as we walk briskly in the cold. She is always
the hand intertwined in mine.
I like her hands on me.

She is her.

I love her.

Why I Love the Rain

There was this one perfect day. It was raining. This was not a simple rain; it hit hard. This was the kind of I'm-taking-a-shower-while-clothed-and-outside rain. This was the kind of rain that sent knives shooting out of the cement in splashes. This was the kind of rain that reminded you of your most primal humanity as it backhanded you in the face. That's what made it magic.

That's what made it perfect. That's what made us toss our cares out the window. We knew we were getting soaked; so who cared?
We went to an amusement park, just the two of us. Owing to the savagery of the downpour, it was deserted. The spooky, empty fairground type deserted. That's what made it magic.

We didn't wait in line for rides. We walked hand in hand, lost in a child like fantasy. Rain drops dripped onto our faces while we kissed. You braved your fear of heights. I nearly threw up, taking the most thrilling ride again and again. And again. I lost count of the hours. I lost track of how cold I was. Sodden hair clung to our faces as we had this wonderland to ourselves. We knew this would never happen again. That's what made it magic.

Whenever I look out the window at a rampant rainfall, all I see is the glow of a carousel. All I hear is the shriek of your laughter. All I feel is love. That's what makes it magic.

My dearest child

My dearest child,

Her name is Nikki and she was supposed to be your mother. I'm grief stricken to tell you that neither of us are fortunate enough for this to be the case anymore.

Her body was going to offer you a beautiful, nurturing home. Her body was going to sustain you, to cherish you, to tend to your every need. She was going to furnish your first house; warm you at the hearth.

She was going to share her life force with you—that is how much she loves you. She was going to water the garden that is you from her own cup. The tenderness and care that she harbours within her is actually visible to the human eye. It is yellow, vast, and as wide as the horizon.

I've never met you, but I miss you. I miss the parts of you that were going to be a reflection of her. I miss the parts of you that were going to wildly grow, ferocious and independent like her. I miss the bravery that I know you would have modelled off of her.

One day, when you exist slightly differently, I will take the lessons I learned from her. I will radiate her kindness to you. I will let you be free and feral. I will safeguard you in a lush forest of kindness. While I cannot be her, I can relay to you the impact she would have had. In a way, she will still be your mother.

My dear child,

I will water the garden that is you from my own cup.

Traditions

Families tend to have traditions,
and we had made a tradition of our very own;
a new tribe blossoming.
Every December we went to a festival of lights;
wandered together, fingers interlocked,
marvel,
admired how the colours and sparkles
glinted off each others skin.

The first year as we left,
it started to snow.
Her first time seeing this white magic with me;
she squealed and kissed me right there,
a backdrop of Christmas lights and snowflakes
framed two silhouettes that merged into one.

A year later she led me up a busy street blindfolded,
my trust tightly clenched in her hands.
I didn't care where she was taking me,
I just knew that I was bewitched
and would follow the echo of her footfalls.
Cars whistled past, and I could hear the brushstrokes
of boots striking wet concrete.
We stopped and she gently turned me clockwise,
traced my skin with her warm hand,
and drew the blindfold down.

In front of me was a building adorned in stars,
a bonfire of lights strung from pillar to pillar.
The beauty of it struck me square in the chest
where her hands met as she hugged me from behind.

So it only makes sense that,
our small family now fractured,
the lights dimmed;
a damper put on the magic:

Christmas will be a little darker this year.

Nikki

Speak her name:

roll it around your tongue,
feel the atoms vibrate
around it,
feel the energy spark
on each syllable.
You put them all to shame my love;
in the darkness
I hear sensuous whispers:

"Nikki."

Your mother had a feeling
when you were a newborn
when she gifted you this name.
She knew you were different,
she knew you were exceptional—
there was a certain lucidity
in her choice.

What a name
to shatter expectations
to challenge perceptions
to go beyond barriers.

You are anything
but plain.

I Don't Believe

I don't believe;
I'm not religious.
I don't believe in a man parting the oceans,
healing the lame and the blind.
I don't believe in a man who feeds the many
with mere loaves of bread,
who changes water to wine.
I don't believe in reversing the drought,
in Adam and Eve.
I don't believe in a virgin birth,
in stilling a storm with the wave of a hand.
I'm not a prophet
but I swear to you:
on that last night,
fairy lights aglow
during that last, shuddering orgasm,
under her loving hand,
in the finality of it all,

that's when I saw God.

Grief

and

sadness

Parallel

I saw myself,
sitting on the floor of a wide open living room.
Morning sunlight filters in through the window—
I'm wearing your t shirt and my messy hair.

You swoop into the room and plant a kiss on my face,
a tea cup in my palm,
and you smile.

Maybe we go to a market
and maybe we stay inside all day.

There's a small baby on the floor next to us
and I'm still so proud of you for carrying her.
My grandmother cried when you told her
that we were naming her Clare.

You're making eggs
and avocado toast
because this is what we have every weekend.

I open my eyes
and I saw myself,
sitting on the floor of a wide open living room.
Morning sunlight filters through the window—
I'm wearing your t shirt and my messy hair.

      I can see small particles of dust in the sun beams
      I watch them twist and spiral and swoop;
      my body creaks as I get up to make my own tea.

      Maybe I go for a walk
      and maybe I lie in bed all day.

      There's a notebook sprawled on the floor next to me,
      my sorry words are what I carry everywhere.

My grandmother cried when they told her
that we didn't make it through.

Dear Devil

The devil's moon smiled down on us
as our souls were howling a lament;
for the loss of each other was an evil so pure,
it was darkness more opaque than the shadows
who insulted our misery.
Something unspeakable was ripped from my body that night,
torn out through the screams and convulsions
dissipating on our breath.
You had to pull the car over
and we wailed
i'm sorry,
i'm sorry,
i'm so sorry.

Dear devil, please have mercy.

Far away

It was an earl grey morning;
the sands bled and wept
and the ocean sang its melodic tune.

The wings of this aircraft
bent under the sadness
of carrying me far,

far away from you.

Grief

The reason i grieve so deeply for you
is a direct measure of how profoundly we loved.
Had we not loved each other so,
our grief would be nothing,
a trivial matter of sheep.

So i do not shy away
from this ocean abyss of grief;

I let it embrace me,
I let it slither across my skin,
I let it whisper sin to my soul,
I open my cracked heart to it—
I let the blackness pour in.

The sheer ferociousness of that grief
is the same measure of my love for you.

And how I love you so.

It Fits Perfectly

It was Monday October 24th.
I was sitting on the floor
Excitedly wrapping 30 presents for her 30th birthday tomorrow. A cacophony of
wrapping paper, small silver bags and stickers littered the floor; all my creative
energy focused towards making her happy. My energies vibrated with an all
consuming love for this woman.

I heard a key in the lock; she shouldn't be home yet. She doesn't finish work for
several more hours. What an incredible surprise, she's come home early.
I jump up, and call to her in a fit of giggles:
"Don't come in yet! Your presents are all over the floor!"
She waits as I dash around, tossing gifts into a basket and throwing an old towel
overtop.

Something seemed off as she entered.
I kept chattering on about tomorrow.
She went to the washroom.
I didn't notice her silence.
She walked back into the living room.
She looked at me, and three words fell from her mouth.
By the look on her face, I already knew.

"I'm so sorry."

I'm not sure what happened then.

Legs collapsed, tears flowed, we clutched each other harder than ever before. We
wanted to take each other's pain away, while feeling incomprehensible agony
ourselves. For this is how we have loved each other—wishing to dull the other's
pain even when our own is too great to grasp.

"I was going to propose tomorrow."

So we take the most sorrowful drive of our lives,
out to where the ring was hidden;
for when I had conspired a birthday treasure hunt for her along with her best
friend,

I was the one being conspired against. The hunt was for me, and this ring and promise of love everlasting was to be at the end.

I tremble as I see that perfect little box,
but when I see the silver, with words that I had written for her engraved upon it,
that is when the earth falls out from underfoot.

"I have found where I belong,
I belong by her side, enduringly."

It fits perfectly.

Dreams

Nightmares do come true.

Perfume

"People can detect at least one trillion distinct scents."

"Smell is the sense most linked to our emotional recollection."

"The thalamus sends smell information to the hippocampus and amygdala, key
brain regions involved in learning and memory."

Sometimes I smell her on me.

Someone walks by wearing a similar perfume
and
I'm immediately transported

to a small apartment in east Vancouver
right before we go out
and you look…

divine.

You smell like love
and you smell sweet.
I could never describe it,
but I could always identify it.

Every time.

She was everything
        she was
my kinda tribe.

My heart hangs heavy in my chest tonight
        my shoulders sag a little lower than they usually do.

Someone wore a similar perfume today as they walked by;
        it was but a split second
but now

I miss you a little harder tonight. I miss you.

Hell

So, we decided to part.
Let go of each other's hand,
and walk through the gates of hell together.

Don't Take Her

Crucify me,
nail me to the cross.
Torture me,
rip out my nails
one
by
one.

Slide your blade down my skin,

slowly.

Paint my face with milk and honey
and send in the flies to feed.

Confine me within the iron maiden,
tear out my lecherous tongue.

Tie your most elegant noose
and snap my neck in two.

Fasten ropes to my wrists and ankles,
wrench me in every direction
that the compass has to offer.

Do it all, do it exquisitely.
Make it dazzling, make it last.

But please;
please, I beg you,
don't take her.

For that is a pain I cannot bear.

Devil's intentions

The devil sits on both my shoulders,
whispers through both my ears,
and thoughts pirouette through my head
riding waves of self doubt.

Why did her words become so impersonal
as soon as she decided to cut off contact?
The reasoning spoke not of I love you's
but rather simple words of practicality.

I asked if I should hold onto hope,
the devil told me to hope.

She told me not to.

I always listen to the devil.

Letting Go

When I let go, I don't simply leave claw marks.
I leave gashes in steel, I leave limbs torn from sockets,
I leave carnage.

I leave fragments of my nails and fingers embedded in whatever remains.
I thought it was because I love hard.

But when you cut off contact, when you told me you needed to heal;

my heart ruptured and

I simply let you go.

I didn't want you to get cut. This time, I didn't want to leave carnage.

And that may be an example
of the hardest I have ever loved.

Packing

I have become an expert at packing
homes, feelings, thoughts.

4 times we moved,

out of your apartment into mine,

out of my apartment to ours,

out of our apartment to your country.

from your country back to mine,

alone.

I have become an expert at packing.
homes, feelings, thoughts,

all packed neatly away.

Sandcastle

I sat like a proud child
in front of the sandcastle I had just built.
All of this, for you my love!
I will build a whole new world with you,
for you.
I never saw it coming
until it was too late,
my sandcastle, crushed underfoot
back to the limp form of the Earth,
as it had started.

Seeing Red

It was mid February in Vancouver and
you used some sort of witchcraft
to turn an old bed sheet and a tangle of christmas lights
into a safe haven in the living room.
It was there that
you painted my body in kisses
red lipstick coating my arms, back, legs, forehead, eyelids, my knees;
you gifted me a visual representation of the love that you had for me.
My whole body encased within the brushstrokes of your lips,
all I could see was red.

Texting you during the days was like
putting my shoes on before I step out the door.
I didn't even realize I did it,
until one day I was left walking in bare feet.
Ink isn't enough to capture the feeling
when someone who has touched your spirit
slips out of contact.

Like shrapnel, little pieces of you exploded into my soul;
became embedded within my skin.
Leaving small scars, maybe not noticeable to others;
but I feel them.
Never fully gone,
fragments of your spirit swim within me;
I, your river Styx.

The midnight lights of Ottawa catch the gleaming silver surface of my engagement
ring.
It sits open in its box, on the window ledge,
a bittersweet reminder,
that even a lifetime wouldn't have been enough with you.

And each night, when I close my eyes and can't sleep,

all I see is red.

Ghost ship

The moonlight and the cold
reflect on the lake.
It's dark outside
and it's dark inside.
The ghost ship of our relationship sails by,
an omen to what could have been.
Pale sails outline the silver horizon
like a white flag;
we surrendered to the distance.

Can't you see
that we are bound together?
Or is it too dark outside
and too dark inside
to see that?

Please point that figurehead back in my direction,
find your way back to me;

don't let me go down on this ship.

Idealist vs Realist

I was the idealist, you were the realist.
There was always hope, there were always more steps to explore.
There were wedding bells ringing, there was delaying the inevitable.
There was the deepest form of love, there was co dependence.
There was heartbreak, there was heartbreak.

There was always love.

Swan Song

I think the angels pity us.
Wilted wings
mourn the loss of us.

We mourn
the loss of us.

Halos removed,
heads bowed in respect
as we march down this last path.
A heavenly chorus
sings our swan song.

Where is the light at the end of this tunnel?

Did they forget to teach us
that it doesn't exist
once your soul has been

r
 i
  p
   p
    e
     d

from your body?

Tears

Her tears
are immaculate
are precious
are something
not to be wasted.
Please world,
don't laugh in her face
as you have mine.
Don't make her cry
as you have done to me.
Her tears
are immaculate
are precious
are something
not to be wasted.

All I could

I know that I did all I could;
this is what sustains me.
I told her I loved her,
I asked her to move in with me,
I packed up my entire life
and moved to the other side of the world,
to her world.
Because
fuck
playing it safe.
I watched the fire in her eyes
turn to unbearable heartache.
But I promise you,
darling, wonderful woman,
I did all I could.

Better

It's 1:09 am
and all I can think of is how
I could have slid my hand across
that space in the car
and lay it to rest on your thigh
more often than I did.
I could have listened more open heartedly;
I shouldn't have interrupted.
My stories seem so irrelevant
knowing that I missed some of yours.
I should have done the laundry more often,
lit candles just for when you came home.
I should have made the bed more than I
did;
I shouldn't have complained
about your night shifts.
I should have gotten ready to go faster
and not been the cause of our
perpetual lateness.
I should have been better
at getting up in the morning.
It's 1:16 am
and all I can think of is how
my hands are shaking,
these thoughts will always haunt my skull,
and I wish I'd been better.

What could have been

I don't wear the ring anymore,
but sometimes at night when I sit alone,
I pick up the box and open it,
contemplate what it means.
Each time I gaze upon that perfect silver
etched with words of rapturous love,
a slow shiver of shock runs up my spine
and I think about what could have been.

Questions

Why is it easier
to light myself into glorious flames
than to heal?

Why is it easier
to tear open
than to sew shut?

Why is it easier
to alter my consciousness
than to stare reality straight
in its
ugly
unyielding face?

A Note to Everyone

Don't
        EVER
ever ever ever ever
promise someone
who wholeheartedly believes you

        "I will never break up with you."

unless you are
absolutely
one hundred percent
without a doubt
Earth shatteringly
        certain
within the pits of your being

        that you will not break your word.

Red Wine

You've stained me.

you're red wine on my teeth
you're red wine on the carpet
you're red wine on my dress
you're red wine everywhere,

Why did I wear white today?

Goosebumps

You were
the witness to my every goosebump:
each soft breath onto my skin,
each time you held me as I was cold,
or saw my eyes light up in wonderment,
you were the sole witness to those tender moments.

How many nights must I lie still,
wrapped in your t shirt,
grasping a pillow and pretending it's you,
before the realization
that you aren't coming back
sets in?

When I think about it I am chilled to the bone;

    these are the goosebumps you'll never see.

Dandelion

An unappreciated, beautiful yellow.
We were a beautiful yellow.
And, as dandelions do,
the yellow fades,
to a simple period of transition.
The white puffs remain to delight
and spread new life.
The saddest part is,
while the little seedlings cling so hard,
a sudden breeze
can break everything apart.
And while they grow anew,
they must do so
so very far from one another.

Ex

We met at a crossroads,
a place between homes.
I thank my lucky stars
that our paths did not run parallel,
destined to never meet.

Instead,
we met at a brilliant
explosive
radiant
intersection.

Two lives at overlapped
in Vancouver:
X marks the spot.

And yet I never wanted to
or thought I would have to
associate you
with the word
ex.

Hope

They say that hope dies last,
when the last breath shudders
from a broken ribcage;
hope leaves within the final wisp.

When you left me,
hope sank its claws
deep,
deep into the flesh of my brain
for it knew the shadow of death
was near.

Hope clung hard.
Hope held on during the nights
when tears puddled
making rivers of my pillow case.

Even when you told me not to hope
my body rejected the idea,
did not understand
why my soulmate wanted to work
towards a future without one another.

Hope clung hard and as
I shook and shook
trying to dismantle it,
those talons shredded apart
little ridges and dips of my
soft brain.

I'm too soft.

They say that hope dies last;
is that
why I can't kill it?

Not Enough

You loved me so much,
and so beautifully,

but not enough.

and that's where our story ends.

But I know responsibility is mutual.

Anger

House on fire

I made a home of a burning house.

I must have been the flint,
and she was the steel.

Sparks were flying the second I walked through that door.

I lay there complicit, in a bed of embers
none the wiser.

Flames licked the four posts of the bed,
a beast hungry for impending doom.
The iron began to sweat.

Being so blind,
you'd think my other senses
would peak,
would realize that the walls
were melting around me.

When I went home for Thanksgiving,
I must have left gasoline in my footprints
on my way out the door;

because when I returned
the whole place was ablaze.

It ended with nothing but ash.

Ash running through my fingers,
no matter how hard I clenched my fists to stop it,

It just drifted away.

Rewind

Three years later
You returned to what you had run from;

during the in between
you found a country that accepted you exactly as you are
and a woman who would give her life to you.

You went back to the exact state that you desired to escape,
And you sent that woman back to her country.

The Hard Truth

The hard truths in life are like paper cuts,
they're like splinters caught in your finger,
they're a headache during an important meeting.
The hard truths in life aren't always visible to others,
they don't wait for the right time,
and to us they hurt.
Our hard truth turned out to be two countries;
Canada and Australia.

How does one reconcile the fact that our families
live on polar opposite sides of the globe?
That's the hard truth.
There is no changing it,
it was set in stone long before we met,
chiseled into the bedrock of this planet we call home.

As you grew up under the sun,
and I grew up through harsh winters,
the Earth agonized and laughed at what was to come.

Two soulmates would fall deeply in love,
would envision a life together,
would not imagine a world within which they didn't exist
together,
then they would be ripped apart.

And so it goes,
hard truths come to fruition.
The tides still come in and out,
the moon still rises,
and my heart beats a little slower.

That's just the hard truth,
on a hard planet,
that does not bend to the softness of others.

Road Map

My love will saturate,
my love will seep into the cracks
and bind.
My love will carve out stone
when given enough time.

My love will inundate,
will flow,
will consume.

You lost yourself in it and left

but you always knew that this is how I love.

I left you a road map
that you decided not to follow.

You didn't

I was handed your terms.

We were equals in our relationship
but when it came to the end,

all was catered to you.

You decided with my mother
when
I would fly home.

You told me not to contact you for 3 months.

I was handed your terms;
an unsigned contract.

You language became completely dispassionate:

"You always have my positive regard."

could it get less personal than that
could it be less intimate than that
could it be more disconnected
from our relationship than that.

You were **already** trying to make space for yourself.

I asked for one thing.
After 2 years
I asked for one thing:
let me know when you receive my letter.

And you agreed, you promised to
let me know when you receive the envelope
into which i poured my liquid heart,
in which I sent my unconditional love.

You didn't.

I had to ask your mother some time later;

she told me you had received it
days ago.

That was a blade to my heart,
that was a bruise,
deep purple,
spreading over my skin.
Blooms of dark violet,
covering my body
in agonizing flowers.

Your mom said you hadn't had time.

This is something I have never bought into.
This is something that is sensitive to my soul.
This is something that you know hurts me.

It takes less. than. a. minute. before. bed. to. tell. me.

But you didn't.
You asked your mother to tell me
(which she also didn't. I had to ask).

This calls into question
if you were ever going to
honour your word at all?

You didn't.

Gone

She's gone now too.

She is different, she is so different.
She's not like any of them, she's not like the wickedness of the past.
She's so much more. She was the future.

And yet the result is the same.

Like everything I've ever known,

she's gone now too.

My Heart Bleeds

Some of my most maddening sadness
stems from knowing you're in pain
for when your heart cries,
my heart bleeds.

The thought of my pain
must be too much for you

so you made up your mind;
you closed the door
you won't picture me in pain
you won't acknowledge me.

I need to pick up my pieces
and pick you up
and off of that pedestal;

I can't even feel angry
that you didn't tell me when my letter arrived
because the second I imagine your sorrow
I break again.

I see you as

embodied perfection.

But neither of us were perfect.

One Knee

There was an invisible mark of hesitation
in her voice
when we spoke about our wedding.

I could sense the slight hitch
of trepidation in her speech
as I brought it up too often.

I applied too much pressure.

Sometimes she wasn't ready,
sometimes she wanted to push it back
another year.

Sometimes I didn't respect that.
Sometimes I was selfish.

Sometimes she avidly planned with me,
excited and expectant.
Sometimes she looked at rings
and said that she couldn't wait another moment.

Once she even asked my parents for permission.

But sometimes,
I could hear some dark creature
in her beautiful,
slightly haunted,
voice.

Sometimes I wonder if I knew
on some level
before she did
that she was trying to
escape a malignant entity,

something that was stopping her
from getting down on one knee.

Take Care

You said there was a problem with our dynamic,
        you felt you had to take care of me.

I had just moved to your country:

No friends.
No family.
No job.

I thought extra support would be a given,
I thought you would be happy to help me
make a home of Australia.
I thought it would be normal to need crutches
        for a little while.

"I felt like this in Vancouver too."

Did you feel like this
during our first year when
I drove you to work and back,
made you dinner every night,
moved you in with me,
held your beautiful head during vicious bouts of homesickness
and
took you home for Christmas ?

Because to me my love
That is just a relationship; that is love;
Give and take.
Support and be supported.

I am not naive enough to be blind
to the fact that you meant
you had to take care
of my emotions.

However, my sweet,
Who held you up

and kissed your face
when finances brought stress,
when bosses wore you down,
when family concerns came up,
when sadness gripped your chest?

Give and take.
Support and be supported.

Now at least
without me,

you can
take care.

Regulate

"I think that it would be good to work with a psych around boundaries…and
regulating yourself and your own emotions."
      — one week post break-up.

Now I'm confused.
Now I'm genuinely shocked.

You *intimately* know
how many hurdles I have obliterated
how many obstacles I have incinerated
how many fences I have shattered
with my 'psych' over the past two years.

You know her name,
you've joined me several times
in her office.

You know how many boundaries I have put up
and how much work I have put in
(and continue to put in).
You know I'm pro counselling.

Where has this impersonal
judging
language come from?
Why are you pretending that I'm not already
avidly working on myself?

You don't need to call her a 'psych'
when you know her.

You don't need to disregard
every mountain I have climbed;

You don't need to show such apathy
to the progress I have made.

Axe to a Gunfight

I brought an axe to a gunfight,
how unsophisticated of me.

I thought we had all agreed to fair combat.

"I'm staying for the year." I swing
"You're delaying the inevitable." She shoots

So I walk out the door,
axe slung over my shoulder,

how unsophisticated of me.

I thought we had all agreed to fair combat.

Rebuilding

Love Only

Ebb and flow of hurt,
we've both screamed
'Why?'
at silent walls
that don't answer.

In the deepest recesses,
in the catacombs,
below all the desolation,
below all the rubble,
I only have love for you.

Raise the guns in your head
and fire at the open sky.

Fight back against the
sandpaper walls,
sandpaper pillow cases,
staircases to nowhere.

There was a certain glow on your face
during our last night;
I'd seen it before:
Peace.

We told stories of us
all
night
long.

I will always cradle you
in my hands
like a soft peach
with love only.

Scarlet blood drips
onto a pristinely white petal,
cracks run up the walls of our home
like ivy;
the harshness of the world
makes its way into our authentic love;
the dam broke.

damn.
we broke.

Cold Iron Earth

In this void,
this gaping abyss
that lives now in each of us,
that ripples in the emptiness that used to be *us*,
there leaves room to build a new relic;

bring part of yourself that was lost
back.

Dig it up from this
cold
steely
rigid
iron
Earth
and rebuild within yourself,

for now there is room.

Stick with me

All the good,
all that you taught me,
that is what will stick with me.

I came to you as soft clay
and you tenderly shaped me,
you guided my hand
to help me form myself,

that is what will stick with me.

Your giving nature,
your thoughtfulness,
your ability to read me,
your simplicity in hearing me,

that is what will stick with me.

You have formed
an essential part of my spirit.
That is what will stick with me.

You will stick with me.

Revolution

I am a revolution
the turn of my hips is an uprising
you are a revolution
the words matching your intent are a revolt
we are a revolution
our minds clashing are a metamorphosis:
closed minds can fuck off,
open minds can coalesce,
don't ever forget
that you are a revolution.

You are gifted.
You are worthy.
You are valid and fuck those
who do not understand you.
I understand you. I see you
beneath the need to keep busy
beneath the pride in your work
beneath the insecurities
I see you in the quiet night,
sitting alone in bed
and that is when you look like
starlight
and that is when
the shadows that slink
and lie in wait are welcomed:
because they simply can't stand up to you.
They cannot darken you.

I am a revolution
the shape of my lips is offensive
you are a revolution
the curves of your body are preyed upon
we are a revolution
our very nature diverges from what they want to see
closed minds can fuck off,
open minds can coalesce,
don't ever

ever
forget
that you are a revolution.

You are eloquent.
You are intelligent.
You are truth and fuck those
who do not understand you.
You are what is real in this world:
binaries don't exist.
Everything is a
spectrum
Light is
a spectrum
and it is beautiful and
everyone can see it
save those who simply wish to neglect it;
and they are the ones who in the end
need saving.

Not us. Not you.

You are a revolution.

I wish

I wish I could sing
for if I could
I would play the guitar
and sing so sweetly,
sweeter than a honeyed sunrise;
I would light candles
and my voice would drape over you
like a new fall jacket.

I wish I was able
to musically invoke
the right amount of emotion
to tell you how much I love you,
to remind you of a couple of things:
       I will be your biggest champion
       Don't you ever quit on yourself
       Don't you ever direct wretched thoughts
       towards yourself
       You are a warrior maiden
       You are a perfectly polished plum
       We had fucking fun
       We transcended barriers

I wish I could melodically enchant you
to summon such sensation in your chest
to ensure that I can peel back every layer
the layer behind that fear of abandonment
the layer behind the trepidation in revealing
all exploits past,
soften the calluses on your feelings,
to musically invoke
the right amount of emotion
to tell you how much I love you.

Smile baby,
we did great.
I will sing without humiliation
to a future

wherein you are the conquerer
of your every desire.

Rebuilding

"So this is where I leave you
Sitting in a palace covered in gold inside my head
This is where I see you
On a bed of roses when I wanna kiss your silhouette"

—Hayley Kiyoko

I had gotten used to that finicky loose floor board.
It was normal to have to jostle the key in the lock a few times
to get it un stuck.
Small faults that were part of daily life,
with which i was completely happy.

I never wanted to rebuild,
I was as comfortable as one could be.
Life deemed it time to force my hand,
and dismantled everything.
A wrecking ball crashed through my home.

It was only during this process of rebuilding
that I discovered I could correct that floorboard,
re grease the locks.
Things could become easier.
I could emerge from the rubble,
a more dazzling version of my past self.

I thank you.
You contributed the shine to my sparkle,
you are why I could rebuild stronger,
rather than remain bound within the rubble.

It's time to build the house.

So this is where I leave you
Sitting in a palace covered in gold inside my head
This is where I see you

On a bed of roses when I wanna kiss your silhouette

Every memory lives here
within these impeccable walls.
This is your sanctuary inside my mind.
This is where you will always live within me.

Our smiles adorn the walls,
our laughter drifts through corridors,
our kisses are immortalized in portraits.

This castle is built for you.
It honours you.
May you look out over the dazzling sea
and know that oceans cannot stop me from loving you.

The grounds reflect bright yellow
because that colour will always be you.
I lay brick after brick to keep you safe,
to keep you with me,
while the phoenix in me re enters the world.

In my mind, you are nothing but beauty.

So this is where I leave you
Sitting in a palace covered in gold inside my head
This is where I see you
On a bed of roses when I wanna kiss your silhouette

Rest your head my love,
here you are free,

here you are eternal.

La Vie En Rose

You made life soft
through a petal pink veil,
la vie en rose my love.
Baby sheepskins and clouds of bliss;
how could anything be more decadent?
You deserve to have symphonies,
symphonies of adoration
written about you.
I can offer but humble poetry,
and it comes through a soft pink lens
sweeter than your morning mocha.
'Hold me close and hold me fast'
we are
la vie en rose
my love.

Welcome

I slid each dagger
out of my flesh,
one by one.
Blood dripped from them
into a chalice
that I rose to my lips
and drank
heartily.
Each knife was
now unsheathed
from where the world had wedged them;
I strung them together in a circle
And welded them into a crown.
Born from flame
and blood
of my former self:

Welcome to my Queendom.

Acknowledgements

Thank you to my best friend Linda who read these poems night after late night and who always gave me feedback. You made my words feel important.

Thank you to Marianne for always opening (and reading!) my emails containing poem after poem after poem. You encouraged me.

Thank you to Muriel for designing this cover and managing to reach into my brain and put onto paper what I had envisioned. You made this beautiful.

Thank you to Mom, Dad and Mac for being the most supportive family and understanding my love of all things poetry. You are everything.

Thank you to Nikki for being you and weaving thousands upon thousands of words into my mind. I could write infinitely more about you; this is the smallest sample of everything that our relationship was and what I learned from it. You are eternal.

About the Author

Alannah Radburn studied poetry and creative writing at the University of British Columbia where she completed her undergraduate degree in psychology. She is a writer, feminist, and activist for the LGBT+ community. She has participated in several poetry workshops, including those run by Ivan Coyote, and by the Brisbane Ruckus Slam Poetry Community.
Alannah's works are inspired by her experiences in day-to-day life, as well as events that have had a meaningful impact on her. She hopes to reach those who feel isolated in their experiences to offer compassion, empathy and solidarity. She has lived the majority of her adult life in Vancouver and just returned to Ottawa after spending four months in Australia.

Email: alannah.radburn@gmail.com
instagram: @alannahrad

10760487R10058

Printed in Great Britain
by Amazon